Momma Mel and momma Boo got married in a beautiful ceremony with lights and pretty candles and Maliyah the baby toddler coug wore a pretty blue and white dress.

Momma Boo, momma Mel and Maliyah the toddler coug move into their own BIG HOUSE.

Sister
to be

Maliyah is excited to become a big sister and is getting ready
for her baby coug sister Vayda to arrive.

Maliyah loves to climb the stairs in her new house.

Grandma and Papa have a baby shower at their house and grandma decorated with a baby elephant theme.

Maliyah is able to get on and off of her own tricycle now.
Her tricycle has a pink horn.

Momma Boo and Momma Mel love having a big house so they can continue to grow their family.

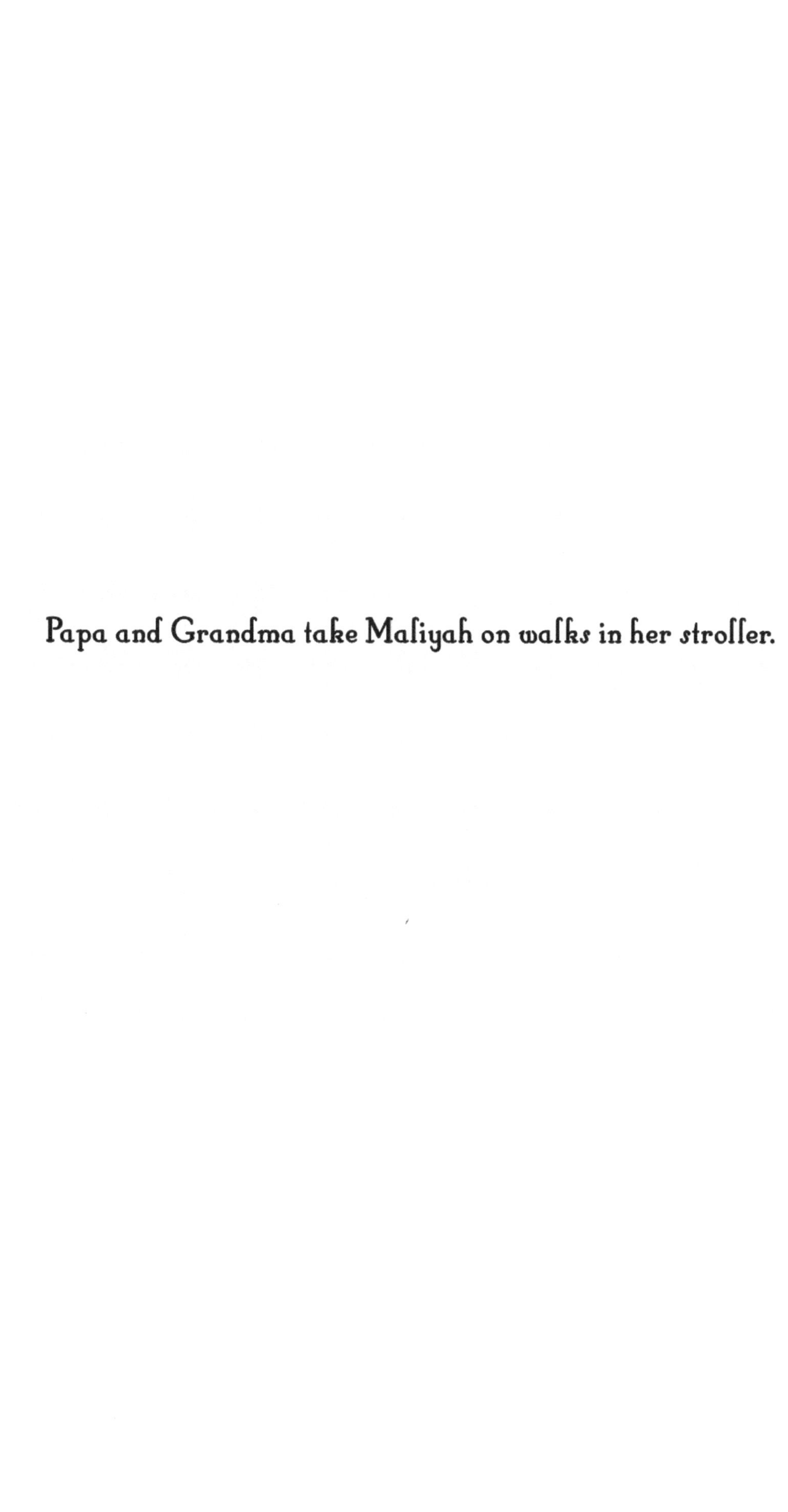

Papa and Grandma take Maliyah on walks in her stroller.

Momma Mel is getting very close to her delivery
date and is ready to add baby Vayda cougar to the G family.

Learning
Spanish

Maliyah is learning Spanish and says "agua" which
means water in English.

Maliyah loves to play with Laila, grandma and papa's boxer dog.

Maliyah loves to jump on her new trampoline.

Maliyah is a very loveable toddler who is going
to be a great big coug sister.